SO, YOU WANT A GOLF COURSE LOOKING YARD

Eugene Weiser
Golf Course Superintendent

1 Fairway at Springbrook GC, Maine

So, you play golf, love how the course looks and want to have a yard that resembles where you play. You want to be the envy of your neighbors. I have written this first part of a series to give you an idea and general outline of what to expect, what you will need to do, and the different things that crop up during your quest for the perfect lawn.

There are many different aspects in golf course care that you will be able to do, while some will require equipment that you can rent, most can be done with the basic tools of general lawn care.

In addition, I will cover general putting green construction and care for those of you that want to undertake this daunting task. While it may seem like a worthwhile task, a backyard putting green will require a lot of care and maintenance that will definitely eat into your playing time. Nonetheless, the ground work will be there.

Before jumping right into the nuts and bolts of bring your yard up to par, so to speak, there are a few basics that you will need before beginning the daunting task of making your yard into the beautiful golf course setting you desire. So, let's begin.

TABLE OF CONTENTS

SOIL TESTING

As a superintendent, one of the first and most important tools I have is the soil test. I don't mean you have to run out and get an expensive soil test done by

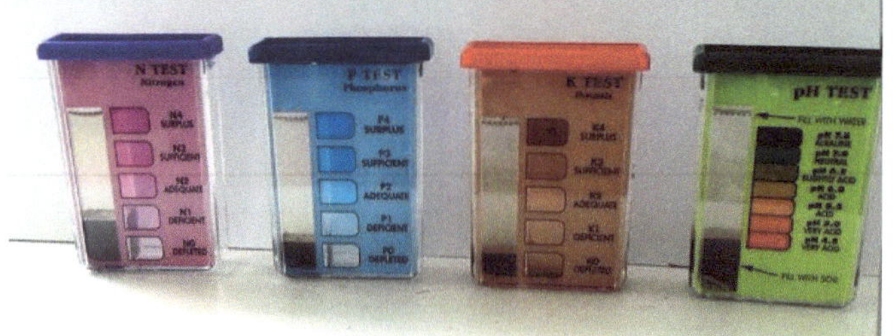

your   **Figure 2 Typical soil test kit**   extension office or university, but a simple testing kit from your local lawn and garden center will be sufficient for your personal lawn. This picture shows a typical home soil test kit that can be purchased at the local lawn and garden center or on-line through one of the on-line retailers. I highly recommend purchasing one of these kits to test throughout the growing season or all your hard work will be for naught. You will also save money in the long run by not needing to apply different fertilizers and nutrients to your soil if the tests indicate there is an abundance of these elements.

Typically, you will have a test for nitrogen (N), Phosphorus (P), Potassium (K), and pH levels. There three elements and the pH test will tell you where your soil is lacking in the proper elements while the pH test will tell you if your soil is acidic or alkaline.

Now that you have your test kit in hand, and have completed your tests, let's help you understand, from a golf course superintendents' point of view, what these results mean for you and your lawn. As noted from above, N-P-K and pH are important for your lawn in many ways. I will describe briefly each one and why you need them. I will also go int briefly how to correct levels.

NITROGEN (N)

Nitrogen is so vital because it is a major component of chlorophyll, the compound by which plants use sunlight energy to produce sugars from water and carbon dioxide (i.e., photosynthesis). It is also a major component of amino acids, the building blocks of proteins. Without proteins, plants wither and die.

Some proteins act as structural units in plant cells while others act as enzymes, making possible many of the biochemical reactions on which life is based. Nitrogen is a component of energy-transfer compounds, such as ATP (adenosine triphosphate). ATP allows cells to conserve and use the energy released in metabolism. Finally, nitrogen is a significant component of nucleic acids such as DNA, the genetic material that allows cells (and eventually whole plants) to grow and reproduce. Without nitrogen, there would be no life as we know it.

The nitrogen in soil that might eventually be used by plants has two sources: nitrogen- containing minerals and the vast storehouse of nitrogen in the atmosphere. The nitrogen in soil minerals is released as the mineral decomposes. This process is generally quite slow and contributes only slightly to nitrogen nutrition on most soils. On soils containing large quantities of NH_4^+-rich clays (either naturally occurring or developed by fixation of NH_4^+ added as fertilizer), however, nitrogen supplied by the mineral fraction may be significant in some years.

Atmospheric nitrogen is a major source of nitrogen in soils. In the atmosphere, it exists in the very inert N_2 form and must be converted before it becomes useful in the soil. The quantity of nitrogen added to the soil in this manner is directly related to thunderstorm activity, but most areas probably receive no more than 20 lb nitrogen/acre per year from this source.

Bacteria such as Rhizobia that infect (nodulate) the roots of, and receive much food energy from, legume plants can fix much more nitrogen per year (some well over 100 lb. nitrogen/acre). When the quantity of nitrogen fixed by Rhizobia exceeds that needed by the microbes themselves, it is released for use by the host legume plant. Therefore, well-nodulated legumes do not often respond to additions of nitrogen fertilizer. They are already receiving enough from the bacteria.

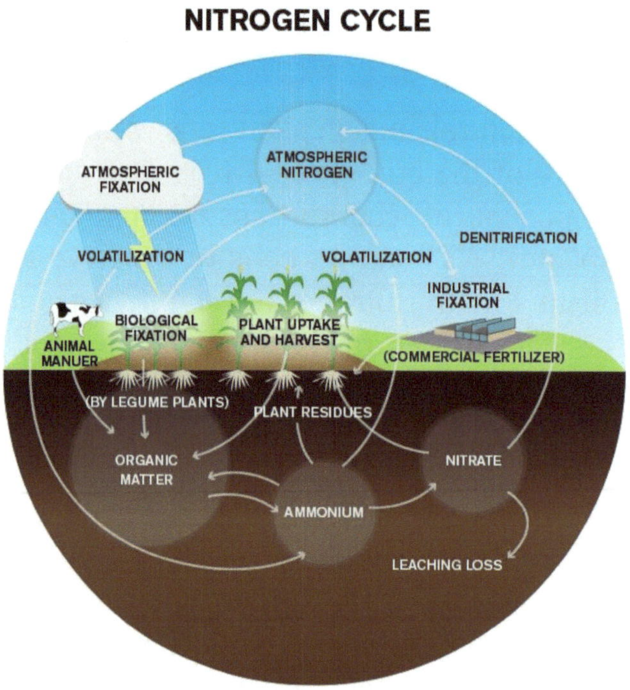

Figure 3 The Nitrogen Cycle

NUTRIENT DEFICIENT SYMPTOMS ON THE LAWN

Deficiency symptoms on lawns usually occur when there is a severe shortage of plant available nitrogen. Visual symptoms of nitrogen deficiencies include:
• Pale green to yellow leaves: This is a consequence of insufficient production of chlorophyll in leaves. Nitrogen is a key component of chlorophyll in plants therefore its deficiency reflects in chlorophyll production. Chlorophyll is the substance responsible for the green pigmentation in leaves and stems.
• Stunted plant growth: A visible sign in a nitrogen deficient soil is the stunted growth of plants. Nitrogen is necessary for cell division and enlargement. Shortage of this nutrient slows growth and development.

There are two ways to effectively increase or decrease your nitrogen levels depending on what your soil test revealed. Generally, your tests will show low nitrogen levels, but on occasion the levels will be high. The only environmentally friendly way to combat this is to balance out your pH levels and not apply nitrogen into your soil until necessary.

Raising nitrogen levels on the other hand is simple provided you follow the recommendations that came with your soil test kit. I will provide details in the appendix if your kit did not come with one or there is confusion. Raising nitrogen. Two ways to raise nitrogen are by using organics on your lawn or by adding commercial fertilizer made specifically for lawns, not gardens unless you want to boost the gardens as well. **Go with a quality, slow release fertilizer.** Slow release or controlled release fertilizers may cost a little more, but in the long run they are the best choice. With slow release formulas, you will be fertilizing your soil less frequently because they are longer lasting. They're also more effective because they release nutrients slowly and steadily.

- Cheaper products can sometimes shock and burn plants, causing a horde of new problems.
- Since chemical fertilizers can negatively affect the soil over time, less frequent applications can help preserve the health of your soil.
- Slow release fertilizers often come in the form of pellets.

The next method is the most environmentally friendly way to raise the levels in your soil, but you will not have control over how much will be added. Composting and animal manure are two ways to go, but not highly recommended for large areas like lawns. You will want to keep this method limited to gardens since run-off may contaminate the water supply or local ponds, streams, or lakes.

PHOSPHORUS (P)

Phosphorus is important for root health and early plant development. Like potassium, phosphorus also helps the **grass** fight disease. Phosphorus is one of the main fertilizer elements (often seen as the letter "P"), the second number of three in the analysis on fertilizers. So, in a 5-3-4 fertilizer analysis, the "3" represents the amount of phosphorus. The higher the number, the more phosphorus. Some phosphorus is needed, and good, especially for roots and flowers.

Since phosphorus is in most fertilizers, moves slowly through the soil, and isn't used in great amounts by plants, there is often an excess. With the potential for water pollution from excess phosphorus, some states and municipalities are promoting (or even legislating) a "no P" fertilization program for lawns. Excess phosphorus causes algae to build up in waterways, disrupting the ecological balance. Phosphorus deficiencies cause leaves to turn purple, creating dark areas in turf.

Recent research has shown that when soils become saturated with water to the point that excess water runs off the site, there is a potential risk that some soluble phosphorus can be pulled out of the soil and into the runoff water. This risk is much higher when soil test levels are in the high to excessive range for phosphorus.

Research has shown also that a dense stand of high quality turfgrass has essentially no soil erosion. Further, it helps reduce total water runoff because of better water infiltration. So if soil test levels become low for phosphorus, such that turfgrass growth and density decline, you could see more phosphorus runoff not less! This is due to poor ground cover from the poor lawn, so increased soil erosion and runoff.

To make sure phosphorus levels are correct, it is important to take a soil test periodically (every three or four years). If the test is high in phosphorus, or greater, there really is no need to add more and there could be environmental consequences if you do. But if phosphorus test levels are low, it is important to provide adequate (not excess) amounts. This will assure good leaf and shoot growth, which will improve turfgrass density, which will in turn reduce water runoff and pollution.

Other methods, in addition to soil testing for phosphorus and using correct amounts, to reduce the risk of pollution from this fertilizer element include:
- Lime to adequately maintain a soil pH of 6.2 – 7.0.
- Apply fertilizer when the soil is dry to moderately moist and lightly water it in.
- Avoid applying fertilizer when the soil is saturated with water or just before an intense rainfall.

- In general, avoid over-watering your lawn. This will reduce the risk of runoff.
- Use a drop spreader rather than a spinner spreader to avoid accidental spreading onto impervious surfaces such as sidewalks and road gutters.
- Avoid mowing such that clippings are blown onto impervious surfaces. Clippings contain phosphorus and contribute to potential runoff.
- Compacted soils decrease water infiltration and, thus, increase runoff potential. If your lawn is subject to a lot of traffic, it may be compacted, and you should consider aerating the soil once or twice a year. This can also help reduce thatch layers.

POTASSIUM (K)

Without potassium, your grass would be stunted and yellowed. Potassium is a macronutrient, along with nitrogen and **phosphorus**. It facilitates the internal processes of the plant's cells, including photosynthesis, respiration, absorption of water and increasing protein production. Potassium deficiency causes leaves to turn yellow and brown on margins.

Potassium is mobile in plants and can be taken up in quantities greater than needed for optimal growth. It can be difficult to identify if overconsumption is a problem because little is known about the optimal concentration of potassium in the turf. Although soil tests are the best way to determine the nutrient requirements of the lawn, in some cases it can be difficult to determine anything more than a potassium deficiency. Plant available potassium is constantly changing in the soil and is dependent on many factors which are interconnected. An overall healthy soil should be the goal with potassium levels falling in line naturally - and with the addition of fertilizers.

Fertilizer blends which are high in K (potassium) are often sold as a winterizing fertilizer due to the potassium effect on the cold hardiness of grass. Consumers need to be aware that terms like winterizer or summer fertilizer are more marketing terms than actual claims of fertilizer benefits.

Now that you have your soil test in hand, you don't need to run out and buy a ton of fertilizer or chemicals. First step is to take a look at your lawn and see where the issues and problem areas lie. Many of these areas can be fixed by simple cultural practices. Areas that have been damaged by pets can be fixed by moving the area where pets go to the bathroom and providing a mulch area of pine needle straw or bark. Traffic areas that have been compressed may need some aeration and a grass species more tolerant to high traffic. If your lawn has an abundance of shade there are a few things that may be done such as limbing up trees (the removal of lower branches to allow air to flow and some light in), removal of smaller 'feeder' trees, or thinning of trees if it is feasible and allowed in your area. There are also seeds available for shade tolerance that may be beneficial. We will discuss the seed selection a bit later.

AERIFICATION OR DETHATCHING OF YOUR LAWN, THE FIRST STEP

Figure 5 Personal lawn dethatcher

Figure 4 2-inch-thick thatch.

Dethatching your lawn is the first step to achieving a beautiful lawn. Many of the nutrients are lost in a heavily thatched lawn and the roots of the grass will tend to remain shallow in the thatch area and will weaken the plant over time, making your lawn more susceptible to disease and summer stress. Figure 4 shows thatch on a lawn that is about 2 inches thick. This will prevent your lawn from growing healthy roots and will block nutrients, water, and air from reaching the roots. When you find thatch 1-inch or thicker or soil that is dry below the surface with deep root growth, it is best to aerate than to just dethatch. Dethatching will work only if your lawn has good roots and not heavily used, but aeration is the best first step. No need to go by weed killer yet as aeration and then establishing a good strong thick lawn will push out weeds. Weeds love touch, shallow lawn with many bare spots.

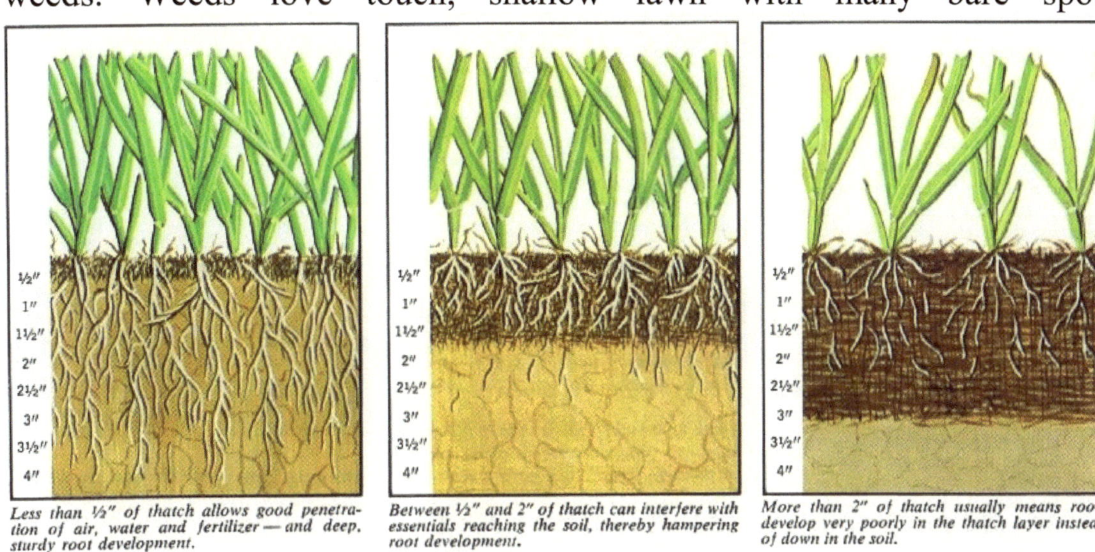

Less than ½" of thatch allows good penetration of air, water and fertilizer — and deep, sturdy root development.

Between ½" and 2" of thatch can interfere with essentials reaching the soil, thereby hampering root development.

More than 2" of thatch usually means roots develop very poorly in the thatch layer instead of down in the soil.

Figure 6 University of Wisconsin description of a thatch build up

Figure 7 shows a lawn aerator that can be found at many hardware rental stores and equipment stores in your area. I highly recommend that you aerate your lawn for the first time as this will allow nutrients, water, and oxygen to reach the roots after aeration.

Figure 7 Home lawn aerator that can be rented at your local lawn and garden or big box rental store

After you aerify your lawn, you will have plugs left all over the lawn. The best approach is to rake the plugs and save them for future use such as filling in low spots, garden soil, etc.

SEEDS AND THEIR USES

PICK THE BEST GRASS TYPE

The type of grass you should plant to withstand foot traffic depends on whether you live in a cool-season (northern U.S.), warm-season (southern U.S.) or transitional (mid-South) grass area.

Cool-season areas: Plant mixtures of turf-type tall fescue and Kentucky bluegrass or perennial ryegrass.

Warm-season areas: Zoysiagrass and Bermudagrass are the two most traffic-tolerant lawn grasses available. Plant sod or plugs of these grasses from May to September to establish a new lawn.

Transitional areas: In transitional areas, neither warm-season nor cool-season grasses are happy all the time. If you will primarily be using the high-traffic area of your yard during the summer, plant Zoysiagrass and overseed with annual rye during the winter. If you plan to use your outdoor lawn area all year, consider planting buffalo grass.

ALTERNATIVE SOLUTIONS

Sometimes, the best practice for high-traffic areas is to forget the grass and use mulch, gravel, or pavers instead. If you're landscaping around a swing set or a children's play area, use mulch. It is softer than gravel and pavers and will cushion the inevitable falls. If an area of the lawn has become a pathway shortcut instead of a green oasis, install pavers, flagstone or gravel. (When using gravel, hammer in metal edging along the perimeter to keep the gravel in bounds.)

A compromise between completely green and completely paved is a stone path with groundcovers such as creeping thyme planted between the stones. These are sometimes called "steppable plants."

PREVENTATIVE MAINTENANCE

Two preventable things cause lawn decline in areas with foot traffic: compacted soil and damaged grass plants. When people or pets walk on the grass repeatedly in the same area, they press down on the soil, which squeezes soil particles together. This means that air and water can't easily move through the soil to reach the grass roots. Eventually, grass grown in compacted soil will die. To prevent soil compaction, rent a punch-core aerator to aerate the grass in high-traffic areas in the spring and fall. Rake a ½ in. layer of finely sifted compost across the aerated area. To prevent plants from being killed by feet grinding their stems into the ground, plant traffic-tolerant grass types.

COOL SEASON TURF GRASSES

PERINNIAL RYEGRASS

Perennial Ryegrass at a Glance
- Cool-season lawn grass
- Fast germination and seedling growth
- Used for permanent and temporary lawns
- Good cold tolerance
- Heat and drought tolerance vary by variety
- Withstands light shade

Perennial Ryegrass Basics

Perennial ryegrasses are used throughout the United States as turf grasses and as high-quality pasture grasses for livestock. Despite its agricultural uses, perennial ryegrass isn't related the rye plant that produces cereal grain. Perennial ryegrass is related to the turf grass known as annual ryegrass, but these two plants differ, too. As the name suggests, annual ryegrass is a short-lived grass used to provide quick color, short-term erosion control or temporary stability for a single season. Turf-type perennial ryegrass is also used in those ways, but it establishes a permanent lawn that comes back year after year in proper climates.

Perennial ryegrass is a cool-season grass, meaning it peaks in growth during cool seasons, from fall through spring. Like many common turf grasses used for permanent northern lawns in the U.S., perennial ryegrass is native to Europe and Asia[1]. Though it's not as cold-hardy as Kentucky bluegrass or tall fescue, perennial ryegrass flourishes where summers are moderate, and winters are cool. In the cool, humid Pacific Northwest, it has become one of the region's most widely used permanent lawn grasses, on its own and mixed with other cool-season grasses.[2]

Even though perennial ryegrass is naturally suited to more northern climates, southern lawn owners use it extensively as well. Warm-season grasses used in the south and west, such as Bermudagrass, go dormant and turn brown during cool winter months. Perennial ryegrass is often seeded over existing warm-season lawns in fall, just as you might overseed a thinning northern lawn as part of your fall lawn tasks. Fast-germinating perennial ryegrass creates a temporary green lawn for winter months, and then dies out when southern heat returns, and warm-season grasses turn green again.

Figure 8 Beautiful ryegrass approach to the green

OTHER CHARACTERISTICS TO CONSIDER

Given the proper conditions, perennial ryegrass germinates faster than any other common lawn grass seed.[3] Once established, however, it spreads slowly. Unlike aggressive Kentucky bluegrass, which spreads by underground stems

---

[1] Duble, R.L., "Ryegrass, Temporary Sports Turf for the South," Texas A&M Agrilife Extension
[2] Cook, T., "Perennial Ryegrass Lolium Perenne L.," Oregon State University Department of Horticulture.
[3] UC Statewide Integrated Pest Management Program, "Grass Seed Germination Rates," University of California Agriculture & Natural Resources.

called rhizomes, perennial ryegrass is a bunch-forming grass. Like tall fescue, it naturally grows in clumps and spreads through vertical shoots known as tillers, rather than spreading by rhizomes or horizontal above-ground stems, known   as   stolons.

Traditional perennial ryegrass varieties have relatively shallow roots, which historically limited their tolerance for heat and drought compared to tall fescue or deep-rooted warm-season Zoysia grass. However, improved varieties of perennial ryegrass, have greater heat and drought tolerance. These improved varieties also require less mowing than common perennial or annual ryegrasses do.

Perennial ryegrass is also a key component in cool-season grass seed mixes for northern and transition zone lawns and athletic fields. Its fast germination and rapid seedling growth provide these plantings with quick color and stability, allowing slower germinating grasses, such as Kentucky bluegrass, more time to get established. Perennial ryegrass prefers sun, but it will tolerate lightly shaded conditions.

Perennial Ryegrass Lawn Care

The best time to plant cool-season grasses, including perennial ryegrass, is in fall, when cool temperatures and other conditions complement the plant's natural growth. This holds true whether you're seeding a permanent northern lawn or adding winter color for a temporary southern lawn. Likewise, the month-by-month lawn care calendar for perennial ryegrass follows that for other cool-season grasses.

Mow perennial ryegrass to maintain the recommended mowing height of 1 1/2 to 2 1/2 inches. Though this is higher than many warm-season lawn owners are used to, this helps clump-forming perennial ryegrass stay dense and look and perform its best. When planted with Kentucky bluegrass in cool-season lawns, mow perennial ryegrass at the slightly taller 2- to 2 1/2-inch height recommended for Kentucky bluegrass lawns.

Perennial ryegrass has relatively high fertilizer and water needs compared to tall fescue and common warm-season lawn grasses. During periods of heat and low rainfall, and during southern winters, the grass requires frequent irrigation to maintain color. If the grass is allowed to go dormant during short periods of drought, it will recover quickly; however, overseeding may be needed after prolonged drought.[2]

Perennial ryegrass adapts well to a wide variety of soil types and to both acidic and alkaline soils. Soil pH in a range of 5.5 to 7.5 typically supports the best perennial ryegrass growth.[1] Testing your lawn's soil every three to four years can help you keep your soil pH and soil nutrients at optimal levels for perennial ryegrass and other grasses present. Your local county extension agent can help with information on kits and care.

When you need a fast-establishing turf grass for northern or southern applications, perennial ryegrass can provide the speed, strength and color you need.

KENTUCKY BLUEGRASS

For many lawn owners in the United States, Kentucky bluegrass is synonymous with the ideal lawn. When given its preferred growing conditions and proper care, this grass produces a dense, lush, durable lawn that lives up to its reputation. However, Kentucky bluegrass doesn't do it on its own. This grass requires a relatively high level of maintenance to look its best, but results can be worth it. Depending on your grass growing region and your lawn care goals, Kentucky bluegrass may be a perfect choice for you.

KENTUCKY BLUEGRASS AT A GLANCE
- Cool-season lawn grass
- Suitable for northern lawns from coast to coast.
- Excellent winter hardiness
- Some varieties susceptible to heat and drought.
- Limited shade tolerance

---

[1] Hannaway, D., et al., "Perennial Ryegrass," Oregon State University Extension, April 1999.

- Some varieties vulnerable to stress damage.

Figure 9 Kentucky bluegrass field

KENTUCKY BLUEGRASS BASICS

The state of Kentucky lays claim to the nickname "Bluegrass State," but Kentucky bluegrass didn't originate there. Like many common U.S. turf grasses, this versatile, widely used grass is native to Europe and northern Asia.[1] Its first use in the U.S. came as a pasture grass in states like Kentucky, where it still covers the state's gently rolling hills. Often referred to in the grass industry by the initials KBG, Kentucky bluegrass rose to become a premier lawn grass throughout much of the country.

Kentucky bluegrass is what's known as a perennial, cool-season lawn grass. This means it comes back year after year and grows most vigorously during the cool seasons of fall and spring. KBG has the greatest cold hardiness of all the common cool-season lawn grasses. It's used most extensively in northern climates where moderately warm summers and cold winters align with its natural preferences and growth cycle.

---

[1] Duble, R.L., "Kentucky Bluegrass," Texas A&M Agrilife Extension

Compared to tall fescue, traditional Kentucky bluegrass varieties have relatively shallow roots, which typically lead to lower tolerances for heat and drought. Historically, this has restricted the widespread use of KBG south of the challenging transition zone, where higher heat and humidity favor warm-season grasses, such as Zoysia grass. Even so, KBG admirers in warmer areas aren't easily deterred. It's not uncommon to find heavily irrigated Kentucky bluegrass growing in sunbaked lawns of the West and Southwest.

ADDITIONAL CHARACTERISTICS TO CONSIDER

Kentucky bluegrass establishes easily from seed, but it germinates more slowly than some other cool-season grasses. Fast-growing perennial ryegrass, for example, germinates in one-third the time of KBG. Unlike bunch-forming grasses, such as tall fescue and ryegrass, Kentucky bluegrass is a self-spreading, sod-forming grass. Once established, it spreads readily via underground stems (known as rhizomes) to form a dense, thick turf. This aggressive growth habit gives KBG the capacity to recuperate quickly from damage.

Part of the charm of a healthy Kentucky bluegrass lawn is its rich emerald to blue-green color. Add to that its medium to fine texture, and a KBG lawn is both beautiful to look at and comfortable for bare feet. As with other cool-season grasses, Kentucky bluegrass growth slows significantly during hot summer months. During extreme heat or extended drought, the grass will go dormant. However, it recovers quickly with irrigation and a return to normal conditions.

Kentucky bluegrass prefers full sun, but some varieties can do well in lightly shaded areas. Look on the seed tag label of many grass seed mixes, including shade and sun & shade mixes, and you'll find KBG varieties mixed with other cool-season grasses. Fast-greening perennial ryegrass and shade-tolerant fescues complement Kentucky bluegrass's strengths to create versatile, lush, cool-season lawns. Durable KBG is also a regular component of seed mixes for athletic fields.

Figure 10 Well maintained lush bluegrass lawn

KENTUCKY BLUEGRASS LAWN CARE

With Kentucky bluegrass and other cool-season lawn grasses, the best time to plant seed and do major lawn maintenance is during early fall, as KBG growth peaks. Because of KBG's rhizomatous growth, the grass develops thatch easily, which can add to drought stress and potential for disease. Depending on your mowing and care practices, your KBG lawn may need dethatching every year or two.

Wise water management is essential for Kentucky bluegrass lawns. Deep, thorough irrigation helps encourage deep root growth, while shallow, frequent watering discourages it. During normal weather, a typical KBG lawn needs at least 1 inch of water weekly from irrigation or rainfall. During warmer weather and in the transition zone, 2 inches or more per week may be needed.1 While the relatively shallow roots of traditional KBG varieties historically required more water than tall fescue or most warm-season counterparts in similar situations, modern developments have greatly improved water efficiency.

Premium, water-conserving seed can add to your lawn's resilience. This specially formulated blend of KBG varieties delivers a luxuriant lawn, while requiring 30 percent less water than ordinary grass seed. Improved varieties build on KBG strengths with improved drought tolerance, richer color, and dense, durable, compact growth that translates to lower maintenance needs.

Like other cool-season grasses, Kentucky bluegrass should be mowed higher than warm-season grasses. Warm-season Bermudagrass, for example, is routinely kept near 1 inch tall, but KBG should be mowed to 2 to 2 1/2 inches high. During periods of high heat and lower rainfall, recommended KBG mowing heights increase to 3 to 4 inches.

Kentucky bluegrass lawns typically require more fertilizer than tall fescue and other grasses. In alkaline soils, blades can lose their rich green color due to pH-induced iron deficiency. The optimal soil pH for KBG lawns is near 5.8 to 7.0.[2] Regular soil testing every three to four years can help you maintain a healthy pH balance and rich KBG color with the help of quality lawn fertilizers, soil amendments and mineral supplements.

When your lawn goals call for a dense, durable, cool-season lawn with luxuriant color, Kentucky bluegrass may be the answer to your hopes.

KENTUCKY 31 TALL FESCUE

Tall fescue is an important turf grass in the United States today, but that wasn't always the case. Kentucky 31, known in the seed industry as KY-31 or K-31, helped tall fescue grasses transition from livestock pasture grasses to lush, durable, manicured lawns. It is valued for easy establishment, drought resistance and improved heat tolerance over many other tall fescue varieties. If you're in the market for an economical, low-maintenance grass — with a bit of history thrown in — Kentucky 31 tall fescue may be for you.

KY-31 TALL FESCUE AT A GLANCE
- cool-season grass suitable for northern and transition zones
- improved heat tolerance over other tall fescue varieties
- drought, shade and traffic tolerant
- high disease resistance
- bunch-forming growth habit

- low-maintenance and economical

KENTUCKY 31 TALL FESCUE HISTORY

Tall fescue grasses came to the U.S. from Europe in the 1800s. These durable, adaptable grasses gained wide use as "forage" or pasture grasses for grazing livestock. In 1931, a University of Kentucky professor heard about a remarkable grass growing nearby. Upon seeing it, he recognized qualities that improved upon common forage grasses, including green color during cold weather and stability on erosion-prone slopes.

Seed was taken from those long-established Kentucky fields and research ensued. In 1942, the grass was introduced into the agricultural seed market as Kentucky 31, named for the state and year in which it was discovered.[1] It quickly gained favor for use in agriculture, conservation and erosion control applications.

As Kentucky 31's popularity grew through the 1950s, its excellent disease resistance and resilience gained attention. Among those keen on the grass's potential was Brooks Pennington, Jr., who was in the process of shifting Pennington Seed's focus from agricultural products to seeds for lawns and turf.

Today Kentucky 31 tall fescue seed is produced in major U.S. grass-growing regions from Missouri to Oregon, as evidenced on the seed tag you'll find attached to all grass seed products. Economical, easy-to-establish Kentucky 31 Tall Fescue remains a leading choice for low-maintenance lawns that can withstand heat, drought and wear.

KY-31 TALL FESCUE BASICS

Kentucky 31 is a cool-season grass, meaning its most vigorous growth happens during cooler temperatures of fall and spring. Like other tall fescue varieties, KY-31 is best adapted to regions with moderate summers and cool winters. It is particularly well-suited to the south-central U.S. and the challenging turf-growing region known as the transition zone. Where weather runs too hot for many cool-season grasses and too cold for most warm-season grasses, Kentucky 31 tall fescue shines.

Tall fescues generally have greater heat tolerance than other cool-season grasses, but KY-31 offers better heat and drought tolerance than many tall fescue varieties. Its cold tolerance, which is greater than that of perennial ryegrass, also gives it an advantage over warm-season transition zone grasses.

In the years since K-31 moved into the lawn and turf marketplace, many new tall fescue lawn grasses have been developed through research and development programs. Compared to many modern turf-type and dwarf tall fescue varieties, KY-31 has a lighter green color, wider blades and a coarser texture.

OTHER CHARACTERISTICS TO CONSIDER

As with other tall fescue varieties, Kentucky 31 germinates much more quickly than Kentucky bluegrass. Its relatively deep roots, compared to other common cool-season lawn grasses, add to its heat and drought tolerance.[1] Though less shade tolerant than fine fescues, KY-31 is more shade tolerant than Kentucky bluegrass, perennial ryegrass or common warm-season grasses, such as sun-loving Bermudagrass.

Like all tall fescue grasses, KY-31 is a bunch-forming grass that naturally grows in clumps. While creeping grass types spread by horizontal above-ground stems known as "stolons" or by below-ground stems called "rhizomes," Kentucky 31 spreads through vertical shoots known as "tillers," which grow from the plant's base. As result, KY-31 doesn't cause problems venturing outside its boundaries as more aggressive spreading grasses often do.

KY-31 TALL FESCUE LAWN CARE

As with all cool-season lawn grasses, the best time to plant Kentucky 31 tall fescue is during fall's prime growth season. Spring is the second-best time to seed KY-31. Because of the grass's bunch-forming growth, Kentucky 31 lawns develop very little thatch, but they typically benefit from regular overseeding every one to three years.[2] Other major lawn care tasks should also be done during the fall season.

---

[1] Lacefield, G.D., and Evans, J.K., "Tall Fescue in Kentucky," University of Kentucky Cooperative Extension, November 1984.
[2] Patton, A. and Boyd J., "Choosing a Grass for Arkansas Lawns," University of Arkansas Cooperative Extension.

K-31's deep root growth helps protect against heat and drought stress, but wise watering practices build on that strength. KY-31 lawns require less water than Kentucky bluegrass, but more water than warm-season grasses such as Zoysia grass. Deep, thorough, infrequent watering encourages deeper root growth, as do taller mowing heights in times of low rainfall. Maintain KY-31 at tall fescue's recommended mowing height of 2 to 3 inches in normal conditions, and 3 to 4 inches during periods of drought.

Versatile KY-31 adapts to a broad range of soil types and does well with less fertilizer than cool-season grasses such as Kentucky bluegrass. Like other tall fescues, it does best when soil pH levels stay between 5.5 and 7.5. Simple soil testing reveals your lawn's soil type, pH, nutrient needs and whether your lawn needs lime or other soil amendments to restore balance and nutrient availability. Your local county extension agent can help with information on testing and understanding recommendations you may receive.

Though many new varieties of tall fescue lawn grass have hit the market since Kentucky 31 opened the door, this proven performer continues to provide lawn owners with resilient, good-looking lawns. Pennington is dedicated to producing the finest grass seed possible and providing you with premium lawn and garden products, helpful educational resources and, in Kentucky 31 tall fescue, an attractive, economical lawn grass and a piece of lawn care history.

WARM SEASON AND TRANSITION ZONE TURF GRASSES

WHAT IS WARM GRASS?

Warm season grass includes those grass types that will grow best in warm months of spring, summer and fall. Warm weather turf grass varieties include:

- Bermuda
- Centipede
- Zoysia
- Buffalo
- Bahamas
- St. Augustine
- Carpet grass

It is best to do some research on which warm grass variety will do best for your growing region, as some warm season grasses are better suited to some areas over others. You can also consult your local Cooperative Extension

Office for the best warm season grass for your area as well as instructions for planting warm season grasses and care.

Other than tolerance to heat, the main difference between warm season grasses and cool season grasses are that warm grasses go dormant during the coolest part of the year while cool season grasses die as temperatures rise and moisture drops.

HOW TO GROW WARM SEASON GRASSES

Planting warm season grasses is done with seed, sprigs or sod. Plant sprigs or sod May through July and spread seed March through September. It is critical that the roots of warm season grasses have enough time to establish before cooler weather sets in. Begin mowing grass when it is long enough to cut and keep a cutting height of 1 inch for best results.

WARM SEASON ORNAMENTAL GRASSES

Warm season ornamental grasses thrive in warm weather and tolerate extended periods of drought. It is best to cut old growth in the spring down to about 6 inches to make way for new growth, which will start as soon as the soil warms. Warm season ornamental grasses vary in size, shape and color but are used extensively in southern landscapes as focal plants, foundation plants and also as barriers. Unlike cool season ornamental grasses, warm season ornamental grass does not need to be divided as frequently. Popular varieties of warm season ornamental grasses include:

- Switchgrass
- Prairie cord grass
- Perennial fountain grass
- Japanese silver grass
- Hardy pampas grass

BERMUDA GRASS

The Spanish brought Bermuda grass to America in the 1500's from Africa. This attractive, dense grass, also known as "South Grass," is an adaptable warm-season turf that many people use for their lawns. It is also found in pastures, on athletic fields, golf courses, parks and more. Let's learn more about how and when to plant Bermuda grass.

Figure 11 Bermuda grass front lawn

INFORMATION ON GROWING BERMUDA GRASS

Bermuda grass is a cold tolerant, warm-season grass that will grow as far north as Virginia. In warmer tropical areas, Bermuda grass will remain green all year long. In other areas that drop below 60 degrees F., it will go dormant. Ideal growing regions for Bermuda grass include the United States Department of Agriculture Zones 7 through 10. Growing Bermuda grass is easy as long as you have the right conditions. <u>Note – For those that have not planted Bermuda grass for turf or other practical uses, its presence can be that of a weed and is very hard to get rid of.</u>

The best time to plant Bermuda grass is in the spring once temperatures are consistently warm; this is generally in April or March in warmer regions.

HOW TO GROW BERMUDA GRASS

Bermuda is not overly picky about soil type and will even tolerate salt spray, making it a good option for coastal regions. Bermuda grass does well in full sun, but it will tolerate some shade. At one point in time, Bermuda was grown only from sod or sprigs but is now widely available in seed form. For best results, use 1 pound of hulled Bermuda grass per 1000 square feet. This grass sprouts quickly and is very hard to get rid of once it starts growing. Start by raking the area to be seeded until it is as smooth as possible. Make a mixture of equal parts sand and seed. The seed can be broadcast using a spreader or by hand for smaller areas. To avoid skips in the lawn, distribute half the mixture lengthwise and half of the mixture crosswise.

CARE OF BERMUDA GRASS

Bermuda grass care is not difficult. A light daily watering is all that is necessary while the grass is establishing. Once the grass is established, the watering frequency can be decreased, but the amount of water per watering session increased. The grass will need one inch per week if there is not significant rainfall. As soon as the grass reaches 2 inches, it can be mowed with a sharp blade. Mowing will help the grass toughen up and spread. Fertilize six weeks after planting with a complete fertilizer that releases nitrogen slowly. Apply a pre-emergence weed control in the fall.

ZOYSIA GRASS

Are you looking for a hardy, drought-resistant lawn that requires little or no maintenance? Then perhaps you would like to try growing Zoysia grass rather than traditional lawn grass. This thick, hardy grass not only chokes out weeds, but it requires less mowing, watering and fertilizing once it has been established in the lawn.

Figure 12 Zoysia grass on a lawn

WHAT IS ZOYSIA GRASS?

Zoysia is a rhizomatous, warm-season grass that holds up well to a myriad of conditions, including foot traffic. In fact, with its tough stems and leaves, zoysia grass has the uncanny ability to heal itself quite effectively when trod upon. Although zoysia generally thrives in full sun, it can tolerate shade. Zoysia grass has the ability to remain alive in conditions that most other grasses would perish in. Their root system is amongst the deepest for grasses and adapts easily to numerous soil types, from sand to clay. However, there is a downside. Zoysia grass is very susceptible to cold conditions and is, therefore, best suited to warm climates.

In cooler areas, zoysia grass will turn brown and unless or until warm conditions return, this grass will lay dormant. Spring is the best time for planting zoysia grass, and there are various planting methods that can be employed. Some people choose to start by seed; however, most prefer to lay down sod or insert plugs, all of which can be acquired at most nurseries or garden centers. Any of these methods is fine and up to the individual.

Laying sod results in a more immediate lawn and usually requires several weeks before it is able to withstand any foot traffic. The newly sod area should be kept moist until the grass is well established. Sloped areas may need to be secured with stakes to prevent the sod from shifting out of place before the roots have had adequate time to take hold. An alternative to laying sod is the method of laying strips. Strips are similar to sod but are smaller and less expensive. The use of plugs or sprigs is more commonly used when planting zoysia grass. Plugs contain a piece of rhizome affixed with soil. These should be kept moist and placed in holes that are around two to three inches deep and spaced approximately six to twelve inches apart. Lightly tamp the area once the plugs have been inserted and continue to keep them moist. Generally, it takes about two full growing seasons for the area to gain full coverage.

Zoysia sprigs are similar to plugs; they include a small portion of rhizome, root and leaves but have no soil, as do plugs. Sprigs are not as expensive and require less care than plugs, both before and after planting. Sprigs are planted much like plugs; however, they are normally fashioned in a shallow furrow rather than holes and spaced about six inches apart. Sprigs should not dry out; therefore, applying a layer of straw mulch is helpful and highly recommended to retain moisture.

CARE OF ZOYSIA GRASS

Once zoysia grass has established itself, it requires little maintenance. Seasonal fertilizing is usually sufficient. Continual mowing is not a concern with this type of grass; however, when mowing zoysia grass, cut it at a shorter height, around one to two inches. Although there are few insect or disease problems associated with zoysia grass, it does occur. The most common problem encountered with zoysia is thatch, which consists of layers of decomposed roots. This brown, spongy material can be found just above the soil surface and should be removed with a power rake in early summer.

OK, you have everything in hand, your ready to make your yard look like a golf course. You have the information I have given you plus some from your local home center, but where to start. Well, that's the easy part. And it's time to move forward. Make sure you pick a nice day in late, very late winter when the snow's gone and the ground is not frozen. At the golf course here in Maine, we usually start about the end of April to mid-March depending on the winter thaw. In Virginia, we always started just around mid-April. As long as the ground is clear of ice to a depth of 6 to 12 inches, no snow or major frost in the forecast, you are good to go.

STEP ONE

Get out there and do it. Pretty simple. But really, the first step is to dethatch or aerate the lawn. After aeriation, the cleanup process begins. It is a matter of raking all the thatch or cores up and making a pile somewhere in your yard in the back out of sight for future use such as filling low spots.

Figure 13 Before and after aeration from a customer's lawn

This is the hardest part, but the most important part of the process. As stated earlier, proper aeration or dethatching will improve oxygen, fertilizer and water movement through the soil profile.

Since aeration or dethatching and cleanup will take the better part of your day, bring out the irrigation or sprinklers for watering. The average home will put out 1 inch of water per hour. The best sprinkler if you have no irrigation system is the impact sprinkler.

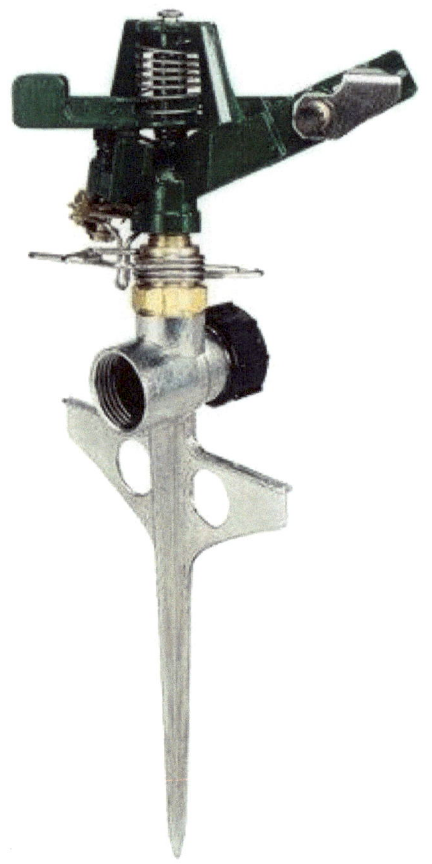

Figure 14 Impact sprinkler from Wal-Mart

The impact sprinkler provides more water coverage per area and can be adjusted to water from 360Degrees all the way to a quarter arc, so you can water just a corner area. Well, that's it for step one, time to shower and rest for tomorrow is going to be a busy fun filled day.

STEP TWO

Good morning and its time to finish that coffee (I have had my 4th cup by now) and get to work. Seeding, watering and fertilizing are our next steps for the day. A fairly short by simple day that plays a major role in your turf. If you haven't already, you should have your seed picked out. I say seed because it is early enough in the growing season to allow growth before mowing and foot traffic become an issue.

SEED AND FERTILIZER SPREADERS

Figure 15 Drop seed spreader

Figure 16 Broadcast seed spreader

There are two main types of lawn spreaders, drop spreaders and broadcast spreaders.

Drop spreaders are made up of a bucket-type container, usually mounted on two wheels, with a raised handle that enables you to push it along as you walk while the spreader releases the seed directly on the ground beneath. Drop spreaders work best for small lawns or areas that need precise applications.

Broadcast spreaders operate by throwing the seed in a swath in all directions. A wide pattern is created so the margins of each pass overlap to provide uniform coverage. Broadcast spreaders require a steady walking speed to ensure even distribution and work best on larger lawns. They are available in both walk-behind and handheld models.

Make sure the spreader is set to the "off" position before adding fertilizer or grass seed. If you don't, you'll waste fertilizer or seed as it is released on the ground.

Set the spreading rate on the micrometer, (this is usually located on the spreader unit near the discharge area) then start walking and pull the trigger to apply. Some spreaders allow you to lock the spreader in the "on" position. **Push forward, not backward**, to avoid applying excessive amounts of fertilizer, which can damage the lawn.
Set the spreader to apply half the amount listed on the label, then make a second pass with the other half.
Fill your spreader with fertilizer on the sidewalk or driveway to prevent fertilizer burn.
Avoid spreading products on a windy day.

APPLICATION TIPS

Irregular shape

- Apply a header strip all the way around the lawn
- Apply product back and forth in the longest direction first
- Make sure spreader is closed when you make a turn
- Steer slowly and smoothly around objects in your path
- Shut the spreader off when you reach the header strip

Rectangular shape

- Apply two header strips across each end so you have a place to turn around
- Turn the spreader off and on at the end of the strip to prevent uneven application

- Before starting back, set the spreader in motion before opening the device in the header area

- Steer slowly and smoothly around objects in your path

- Keep the wheel about 4' from objects you don't want to fertilize

- Overlap to prevent missing an area.

And that's it for spreading. First the seed is spread. After you spread your seed, begin watering in for about 30 minutes to allow the seed to get its first taste of water and to push into your dethatched or aerated lawn.

After the thirty minutes are up, it is time to fertilize. It is recommended to use a labeled product for starter fertilizer as found at Lowes® or Home Depot®. Most will be a 16-16-16 or a 20-0-6 for lawn start up. Remember, **more is not better. Apply only at the label rate.**

Growing in your lawn requires patience. Within two seasons, you will have a lush, green beautiful lawn. And with that, we are not done.

After applying the fertilizer, it's time to water, water, water. For today, apply another 30 minutes of water. This will allow the fertilizer to get into the root zone where the turf will start to feed. Water for one hour, preferably in the early am for one week to establish seed growth and supply more H2O into the soil profile. Do this only for about a week and then it is time to curt back on the water.

STEP THREE

WATERING AND FERTILIZING SCHEDULE SET-UP

A good watering schedule is paramount for a great looking lawn. Most people believe that you must water every day heavily. This is not the case. If you see our fairways and roughs on the golf course, these are generally watered only

2 or 3 times per week, while greens are watered every day, especially in the summer.

Figure 17 Typical Irrigation on golf course

A good schedule for your home lawn is typically 3 times per week, in the early morning or late afternoon hours. Try not to water in the early afternoon when the sun is brightest unless your turf is starting to show signs of wilt (it will get a purplish tint to it), then it is time to bring out the hose and hand water the stressed areas.

Figure 18 Hand watering. Notice the purple 'Stressed' Areas

Hand watering is a practice used by golf course superintendents all over. It is a practice that uses less water, hits only the target areas and doesn't over stress turf that doesn't need the water.

A good point to remember is **MORE is NOT BETTER, Always follow the label rates on the bag.**

Now that that is out of the way, a weed and feed fertilizer is your next step 4 weeks after your first application. After applying the weed and feed, water in for 30 minutes either with your irrigation system or impact sprinklers. Always water in so as not to have run-off of fertilizer into roadside drainage ditches or neighbors' yards. This is environmentally friendly and cost efficient since you won't be wasting fertilizer.

After this application, wait another 4 week and apply a slow release fertilizer to your lawn, sticking with your same watering program. This will allow the lawn to feed and grow filling in the bare or bad areas and out compete the weeds. By now most weeding can be done by hand.

STEP FOUR

THE MOWING PATTERN

Figure 19 A well Stripped lawn

A golf course stripes their turf by repeated mowing in the same direction, though the directions are typically changed daily. We mow by the 'clock' pattern; i.e. 1 to 7, 12 to 6, 3 to 9, and 5 to 10.

In figure 20 this is the 12 to 6 pattern that we follow. It is simple once you do it and looks great.

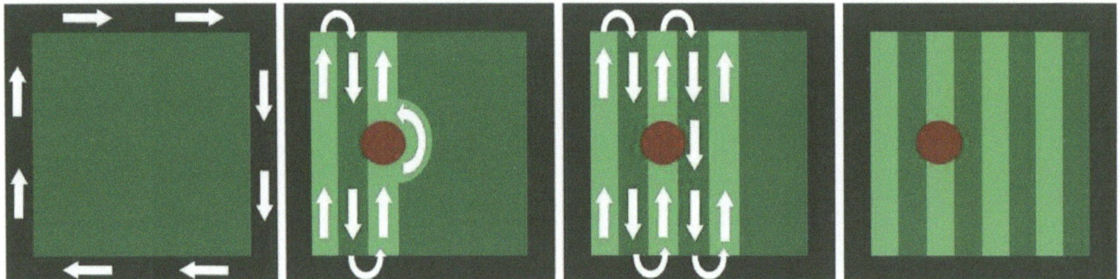
Figure 20 How to mow in a stripping pattern

We mow these patterns for a few reasons. One it looks great, but two, it allows the turf to grow at an even length especially if the direction is reversed every mow. I suggest mowing once a week on your lawn unless it is growing fast, then twice a week except in the summer.

There are attachments you can put on your mower to help aide in deeper looking stripes.

Figure 21 A stripping kit found at your big box lawn and garden store

These kits will allow you to strip your lawn easily and are found at most big box retail stores. They can be homemade as well and instructions can be found on YouTube videos.

A well cared for lawn from spring to fall will allow your lawn to come out of winter looking ready to play on. Do not apply nitrogen fertilizer before winter strikes because this will feed the dreaded snow molds. The big Box stores will have a winter fertilizer to apply and it is recommended to begin applications around November, about the same time you aerify your lawn for its winter nap.

FUTURE SERIES

Future series of this book will include
- Irrigation planning and installation
- Building a home putting green
- Pesticide and Chemical safety
- Turf specific fertilizers
- Outdoor low voltage lighting

If you have any questions or comments, you can reach me at

gene@landscapeirrigationconsultants.com

and my website is www.landscapeirrigationconsultants.com

www.ingramcontent.com/pod-product-compliance
Lightning Source LLC
Chambersburg PA
CBHW040051240726
48664CB00004B/1148